SO THOUGHTS ON SCOUTS AND SPIES

CW00525528

BASED UPON THE

EXPERIENCES OF THE

AUTHOR AND HISTORICAL

OBSERVATION

by
Gerry Barker

Originally published by
Frontier Resources
Edmonton, Kentucky
MCMXCVIII

This edition published by
Greenleaf Press
Lebanon, Tennessee
MMX

The author and the publisher are deeply grateful to
David Wright for permission to reproduce his
painting, "Treed" on the cover.
Further examples of Mr. Wright's remarkable
paintings of scenes from the American frontier can be
found at his web site:
http://www.davidwrightart.com/

Originally published by
Frontier Resources,
774 Delk Branch Road
Edmonton, Kentucky 42129
(270)432-4796

This edition published by
Greenleaf Press

www.greenleafpress.com
1570 Old Laguardo Rd
Lebanon, TN 37087
GREENLEAF
P · R · E · S · S

This work is sincerely dedicated to the SCU who taught so many of us so much and got so little in return.

CONTENTS

APPENDICES

AUTHOR'S PREFACE

Some years ago, in another war, I had the opportunity to watch some tribesmen hunting near their village. Stripped to breechclouts and encumbered only by their tiny bows and the knives at their waists, they moved through the forest as quickly and quietly as the deer they hunted. I was awestruck. As time went on, I saw them at war, as scouts and spies, and as trackers. My poor skills cannot even come close to what I was allowed to watch.

This book is the product of watching other people, of spending time scouting, and some reading. It is not a research work, nor is this intended to tell anyone the right way to do anything; just what I have found by making a lot of mistakes in the woods. I have been lost, caught by the enemy when I did not want to be, skunked by deer, and let my party get far too close to danger. My hope for this book is that it can be a starting point from which better minds than mine can begin to collect a body of information on the skills of frontier warfare. Not just in a book learning fashion, but practical, on the ground information.

This is also written with sincere appreciation to the many people who helped over the years, only a few of whom can I mention here, Bill Durand, Kuska, Jimmy Horton, Dat, Dun, Bushy Leeman, Mark Sage, Jon Hayes, Dan Bergerson, David Wright, Mark Baker, Gordon Smith, and Jeff Wagner.

SOME THOUGHTS ON SCOUTS AND SPIES

Scouting

One of the hardest skills to find in the wilderness is that of the scout, also called a spy. We have heard of them, men like Robert Rogers, Samuel Brady, Simon Kenton, and William Whitley but they are few and far between in any culture. A scout finds the enemy, without being detected. If he fires his gun, he has failed. He moves with freedom in a forest where he knows he has no friends. It is almost impossible to recreate these skills today. These are skills based on fear, on war, and on necessity. This creates a totally different look of frontier life. It is unadorned, uncomfortable, and silent.

The scout itself is a short trip, at most a month, sometimes only a few hours of silent movement. It requires total concentration and complete immersion into the environment. The scout feels everything around him. Often a whole party can pass through an area without so much as disturbing the wildlife, but ---- this ability requires the scout to completely subject himself to his craft.

There are three absolutes in scouting: All around security, silent movement, and concealment. A breakdown in any of these means failure. Time has to cease being the controlling factor. A single quick movement can bring disaster. Silence is essential. Scouts hear an enemy before they see him. You can "listen" your way through an enemy line.

Scouting is the art of finding the enemy without being seen, but there is more to it than that. The scout must also bring back the information in an understandable, organized fashion that can be used by other people. This art is as old as mankind itself and the skills cannot have changed much. It matters not if it were a Roman Centurion leading a squad out to find a German camp or a Captain in the Virginia Militia who seeks a Miami village, the problem is the same. Benjamin Church, after his experience as the commander of Massachusetts troops in King Phillips War, published a set of rules for scouting in 1704. These look suspiciously like Major Robert Roger's rules of sixty years later. It is these timeless elements with which we are concerned.

Preparation

When the leader is told that he has a mission and the purpose of the scout, he must make sure that he accomplishes certain things before he leaves with his party. In a worst case, these may all be done on the run out the fort gates, but to be successful, they all need to be done.

In truth, the more work that goes into the preparation, the more chance of success. The best idea is to start by making up a list of things to do and a time schedule.

Next, the leader need look to his mission, analyze it and develop a plan on how he intends to accomplish it. As a part of this process, he will have to find out all he can about the area he will go into. Has someone else been in there? Are there maps? Can he get out and look at all or part of the area first? How many people will be needed? How long will the scout take? What supplies will be needed?

There are a number of things that the leader should consider in planning a scout:

How large a party is needed? A good man alone can almost always avoid detection. Two people may have a better chance of overcoming hardships but are twice as hard to hide. Three, four, five or six may be necessary if there are a number of things to be done or much to be carried, but the noise of movement increases dramatically. Eight men may be too many to hide and too few to fight. Do not discount the possibility of a one man scout. A single, experienced scout may be the most effective means of obtaining information.

What must the scouting party carry with it? The more supplies carried, the slower and noisier the party will be. Care must be taken to avoid taking too much on the scout. Safety depends on avoiding detection and a heavily loaded company is far more vulnerable than one lightly loaded. Safety does not depend on the party being able to fight its way out of contact with the enemy, but rather on avoiding detection. The scout travels light at the expense of his own creature comforts. For example, if it is to be a short scout, can bedding be limited to match coats or left behind completely and the party huddle together for warmth at night? Much depends upon how long the scout will take.

What should the party wear? Should the company dress like the enemy? Do not mix some in your uniforms with some in the dress of the enemy, but dress everyone one way or the other.

Is a mix of weapons needed? Will they need any tools? An ax, for example, or rope and halters if the leader plans to steal horses?

People must be recruited and organized. Places in the march should be assigned as well as security assignments. Individual tasks before, during, and after the scout may be necessary. Successful leaders ask people to help with parts of the overall task at hand. This permits greater attention to detail. The leader also needs to talk to other people working in and around the area of the scout. Supplies must be acquired, packed and parceled out to the various members.

Some members may need to be taught specific tasks, for example, how to walk flank. All the members of the company may need to practice things that are planned for the scout, such as an ambush or a river crossing for example. Especially difficult or dangerous tasks should be rehearsed as a minimum. This rehearsal may only be a quick discussion, but everyone needs to understand how things will be done. There is no time for discussion when the enemy is in hot pursuit. These discussions or rehearsals may include:

- How the party will move
- What to do if found by the enemy
- What to do at the objective
- How to make camp
- What to do if someone is lost

Everyone should be inspected for appropriateness of clothing, weapons and provisions before departing. In the inspection the leader must make sure the clothing is subdued and nothing will attract enemy attention. He must insure that supplies and equipment are complete, every firelock works and has sufficient powder and shot, also that each man has water and spare moccasins. Finally, he must see that everything is packed securely and will not fall off or make noise.

At some point, when the plan for the scout is complete, every man in the party should be told the whole plan. Thus, if the company becomes separated or the leader be lost, the mission can still be completed.

This whole process may be as simple as an instant consideration of the job at hand, followed by the leader calling for a buddy to join him and to grab his rifle and haversack, telling his friend to follow him and do what he does, then the two of them slipping into the woods. If they have worked together before, this may be a very effective short scout. Going from Ft. Pitt to the Sandusky villages, on the other hand, takes much more work.

THE SCOUT

On the scout itself there are a number of elements to be considered. Scouting is a collection of very specific skills that are far more important than any weaponry or equipment that may be available, or not available. How a party avoids detection by the enemy is more important than their ability to fight their way out of trouble. Often scouting parties are very good about their practices in the beginning but become lax with time, especially on the return march. At this point people begin to talk in normal tones of voice and stop covering their sectors, simply walking along looking at the heels of the person in front of them. This kind of breakdown in discipline loses lives. Even a small scout close to the main body needs to remember who they are and what they are doing. There are also some people for whom being quiet in the woods is an impossible task. They may be effective people in many other ways, but on a scout they are a liability and it would probably be best if they were left behind.

FORMATION

If the party is two or more, a decision must be made as to the formation to be used: Two men can walk abreast or one behind the other. If being tracked is likely to be a problem, single file may be best so the hindmost person can erase the signs of passage. Two columns, staggered, will give better all around protection in a fight but takes many men and it is impossible to cover the tracks of this formation. Flankers may be wise if the party is large, especially if travel on roads or paths is necessary. Robert Rogers thought that it was best to cross a swamp in a line abreast in order to leave fewer tracks. Keep an interval of five to ten paces between people in the woods and twenty paces or more if you have to cross open areas. Oft, it may be necessary to break the party into small groups of two or three and proceed independently to an agreed meeting place. Irish rebels use this technique frequently because all are equally familiar with the land. In any event, a plan must be made and enforced to have someone looking in all directions for the enemy.

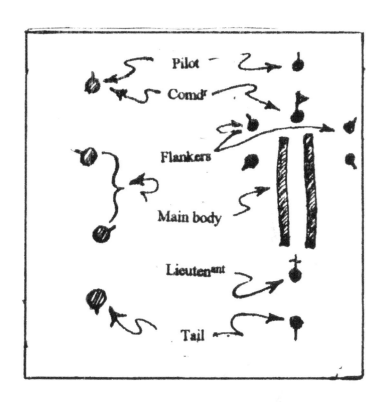

FIG. 1   Four men in line and a Co^y column

THE PILOT

The leading person in the party who acts as spy, guide, often navigator, and most important, the forward security of the company, is most generally termed the Pilot.

Above all, he is responsible to make sure that the party does not walk into danger. He must see the enemy first. If there are side trails or hazards he will generally stop the formation and investigate before continuing. If the enemy is discovered he gives a warning sign and the company can hide or withdraw to avoid detection. If necessary the Pilot may fire to save the party.

The movement of the Pilot must be slow enough for him to observe all dangers as far out as he can see. He looks high into the canopy, he looks at the terrain level, he looks under the undergrowth, and he looks at the ground over which he must move. Most of all, his gaze must cover from side to side and the whole front of the party.

Listening is an important part of this process. A good pilot is so quiet that he can hear the enemy while he is on the move. He stops frequently to listen for things that might be out of place. At each halt he looks back at the rest of the party to get signals from the rear of the column.

There should be a space of ten to twenty paces between the Pilot and the next man. In open areas or approaching an area of increased danger this may be increased to as much as fifty paces. The Pilot needs room to work. His skill may permit him to see and hear the enemy before they see and hear him, but all is for naught if the enemy detects one of the following people in the party.

Many good spies and leaders of scouts seem to like to walk pilot themselves if they are with a small party. If there are two, three, or four in the party this may be a good idea. As the party gets larger this becomes unworkable. The leaders of Indian war parties are most often their own pilots and this seems to work very well for them.

THE TAIL

After the pilot, the Tail is the next most difficult position to work. The Tail is responsible for the security of the rear of the party. As well as observing to the rear, the Tail must cover the signs of movement that are left by the company as it passes. For this reason, the Tail may be left behind accidentally. They become involved in the covering of the trail and the party moves off and leaves them without knowing it. A good Tail will learn how to walk backward silently and is always alert to movement behind the scout. It should be remembered that most contacts will be rear contacts.

Covering the trail consists of removing all signs of passage or so disguising them that the enemy will not be alerted to the presence of the scouting party. Rarely can tracks be erased, but the distinctive track of a shoe pack can be altered to look like two overlapping moccasin tracks. The marks of the seam on white man's moccasins can be disguised. Broken twigs or branches can be hidden. Rocks and pebbles that have been disturbed by the company's passage can be returned to their original place. Grasses should be stood back upright. Bruise marks and hand prints on tree bark can be enlarged to look like blotches. Scuff marks or mud left on rocks or tree roots can be removed or hidden. The Tail should never cut a branch to sweep tracks away; this leaves a set of identifiable marks that look like someone trying to cover their tracks.

At the halt, the Tail must pay special attention to the security of the rear. Rarely will an enemy overtake a scouting party while they are on the move. Instead, they catch up to them while they are taking a break, halted for lunch, or making camp.

FLANKERS

Flankers may be needed if the party is large or travel on roads, or trails, becomes necessary. The most important purpose of flankers is to prevent the party from becoming the victims of an enemy ambuscade. A unit may be flanked by one or more people on each side. They should walk more toward the front of the column, but stay far enough back from the Pilot so that they do not interfere with his work. Flankers cover a sector from the front to the rear of the party on their side.

The position is much like walking pilot and often leaders will use this position to train new pilots. The Flankers move slowly, paying special attention to looking under foliage for ambush positions. If the Pilot is moving at a safe rate of speed there is little danger of leaving the flankers behind. In some cases, if a party must move out at a rapid rate, it may become necessary to pull the flankers in to avoid losing them.

ROUTE

The route to be taken is another major consideration. In general, the more difficult the land, the less likely the enemy is to be looking for a scouting party. The route should be easy to follow, guiding along ridges, paralleling roads or rivers, or aiming at a distant feature such as a mountain or a gap. As a rule, scouts avoid the tops of ridges and do not use a road or path unless the company is strong enough to fight off an ambush. It is wise to return by a different route from the one taken to the objective. The leader should also avoid known dangerous areas such as built up areas, large open areas, &c. It may be possible, however, to use open areas after dark. It is also wise to plan for an alternate route out and back just in case something goes wrong or one of the routes proves to be impossible.

MOVEMENT

The movement of a scout must be silent, slow and cautious. Scouts move a short distance, stop, listen, look over the area which they will move through next, look for sign of the enemy, then move again. Major Rogers' admonition to move like you are sneaking up on a deer is wise. Good deer hunters move like deer. Deer move in short bounds, constantly looking over the area they will move into. Often stopping for long periods of time, deer stand motionless, carefully searching the land ahead for danger. Scouts spend a lot of time looking and listening. They learn to hear the enemy, even a quiet enemy. The scout will stop shy of hill tops or ridges and peer over into the next low space with his head just over the top. Deer use this trick a lot. Scouts must think about the surface they will cross. Is it safe? Is it free from hazards? Can it be crossed silently? Will he leave tracks? He squats down from time to time and peers under the foliage; this is how he will detect ambushes.

Moving silently takes a lot of practice. The scout should look at the area where he is going to put his feet. He lifts the foot high enough to clear any obstacles. He puts it down softly with as much sole surface making contact with the ground as possible, feeling his way down. Steps should be kept short so the spy can always be in balance. When in grasses or vegetation that can be broken down, he slides the foot down gently so that nothing is crushed and as little as possible is broken. With practice a spy can cross a field of tall grass without leaving trail.

While the rustling of leaves cannot be heard a long distance, the breaking of twigs and branches can. If the spy feels a twig under his foot as he is putting it down, he picks the foot back up and works it into a new place. On the frontier, scouts generally do not wear hard soled shoes because they are impossible to keep quiet. The scout works his body between obstructions, trying not to brush any foliage if he can help it and threading his weapon through the openings. To move silently, he must be lightly loaded and his balance must be good because he will be on one leg a lot. All of his equipment and clothing must be very close to his body. Moving in this fashion a scout can move ten to fifteen miles on a long summer's day, but it is hard work and there are almost no breaks.

Wildlife grows quiet when they detect an intruder. The woods will take about twenty minutes to return to normal after being disturbed. If he can move quietly enough, the forest sounds will continue uninterrupted.

NAVIGATION

Finding one's way overland is a major problem for many people. We are just not in the wilderness enough. First of all, a Scout should get the lay of the land. He does not place sole reliance on his map and compass----without an understanding of the nature of the land, maps and compasses can be a liability. Hills and watercourses have a grain like wood. Once this is understood it becomes easy to maintain a course. Thus, the Spy learns that all streams and rivers in the area flow north into Ohio. Even if a creek he encounters runs south for a while, it must eventually meet something that will flow north. Ridges may be scrambled, but the uplands lie on a line from northeast to southwest, &c. On the frontier, few people have either maps or compasses and yet they find their way quite well.

The Spy should not try to be too accurate; moving in a general direction is a better idea, northwest or south for example. He uses the sun, moon or stars to establish north. In a pinch, when a thick layer of clouds completely removes all signs of the sun's location, the direction of the cloud's movement, and knowledge of the weather patterns, will give some indication of west since most weather generally comes in out of the west.

The Scout moves, keeping his shadow at a given angle for a while then adjusting as the sun moves. The wind is generally constant for a day or two; therefore, if it is kept on the same quarter while walking, the Spy will be able to maintain a course fairly accurately. The same can be done with clouds as they are blown across the sky, so there is no reason to feel that an overcast day makes navigation difficult.

He aims at missing his target on a known side so that after traversing a forest he knows he will come to a creek on the south side of the pond he is looking for. This way, when he finds the creek he knows he will turn left to reach the pond.

Spies must study the map before hand; make a plan, then follow the plan. Any person can train himself to work without a map and compass if it is important to him.

If he gets lost, he does not panic. Everyone gets lost. The trick is to pick well defined boundaries (roads, river, &c.) that will keep one in his area and help him get reoriented.
In a worst case he can go out to the boundary and restart.

When using a compass and a map, the Scout must remember that most maps are light coloured objects, easy to see in the woods, and must be used in a secure place. He takes the compass out, orients the map to north, finds his location and picks out his route, then puts the map and compass away. In the absence of any landmarks or identifiable terrain features, Scouts may follow a compass course, but this is a last resort. The Spy can take an azimuth (an angle measure from North) with the compass, pick a distant point to move toward, then put the compass away. Walking pilot with a compass in hand is dangerous and should not be permitted. The Pilot can keep on course by keeping the sun at a given quarter, watching his shadow or the shadows of trees or any of the other methods.

SECURITY

For any party making a scout, success depends upon security. Security is all things done to avoid detection and survive an encounter with the enemy.

Most basic of all is the ability to move without being seen or heard. Clothing should be selected to avoid attracting attention to oneself. Light colors and high contrast fabrics or decorations should be avoided. Often white power horns, or beads, or the brass work on a rifle will give a person's position away. The face, neck, and lower arms cannot be allowed to reflect light. A brimmed hat is one of the best choices because it breaks up the outline, keeps the face in shadow, and gives less of a human look to the upper body.

As soon as practicable after beginning a scout, usually upon entering the woods, the scout should stop, crouch and simply listen and watch the forest. This allows him to become "in tune" with the life and tempo of his environment. It slows movement. The scout becomes a part of the environment. Movement must be silent. Every member of the scout must look to their clothing and equipment to make sure that it is as silent as physically possible. Does anything rattle or clank? Will the powder horn bang against the hilt of the knife? Does the short starter bang against the musket when he walks? *&c.*

All attachments such as horns, pouches, packs, &c., should be worn high and close to the body. On a scout, the ability to move silently far outweighs the need for quick access to powder and ball. A low slung hunting pouch makes noise and is uncomfortable when a scout crouches ten times per mile to look under foliage. A pouch or cup dangling on a belt tends to snag vines and branches making noise. Big offenders seem to be loading blocks and powder measures. Canteens are notoriously loud and should be blanket covered or stored inside a pack or haversack.

Everyone in the party should be prepared to stop and "freeze or take cover" if someone detects the enemy or a possible danger. This requires that every member of the party be completely alert at all times. If the party's concentration begins to falter it is often better to give the party a break to recover their attention.

A major part of security is the ability to detect the enemy before he becomes aware of the presence of a scouting party. This means that someone must be looking in all directions at all times. If a person is alone, he must watch all the way around himself. When there are two people in the party, one watches the front, the other watches the rear. They must make eye-to-eye contact every few steps in order to assure passage of information. When a third person is added, the circle is divided into thirds.

The Pilot is responsible for security to the front, detecting the enemy a safe distance from the company without being detected himself. The Tail covers rear security. Most contacts will actually come from behind. The enemy finds tracks left carelessly and follows the scout, eventually catching up to them when they are taking a break or setting up camp. Flankers are often necessary, especially if movement on a trail or road is necessary.

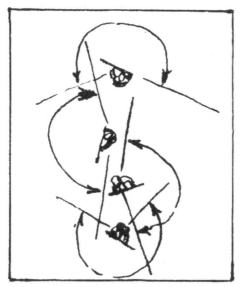

Fig. 2   Security sectors on the move

Everyone else in the party is given a sector to watch, both on the move and at halts. Each sector is said to go from man to man. Thus, if a person's sector is to the left, it goes from the person in front of him to the person behind him on the left side of the column.

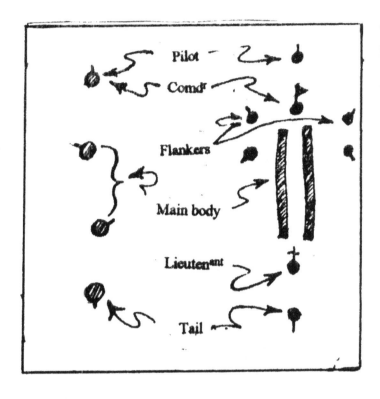

Fig. 3   Security sectors at a halt

At a halt, each person should take cover, automatically stepping into their sector and using a tree, bush, or rock *&c.* to hide behind. When setting up a camp, sectors remain as they were on the march until the leader makes new assignments. When a camp is made or any sort of hazard encountered it is often a good idea to send a small scout out to ensure that the enemy is not close. In some cases, outposts should be posted to protect the approach to the camp.

In all cases, sentries must be posted. History is filled with examples of parties being surprised in their camps. Having more than one sentry gives assurance that should one sentry become distracted or fall asleep there are other sentries on the alert.

The number of sentries actually needed in the dead of the night, well off any trail or traveled way, may be debatable, but a party should never rely on a single sentry. Many leaders, Robert Rogers among them, advocate that half the party should be on guard at any given time.

Finally, it is wise to arrange for emergency meeting points called "rallying points" or sometimes "rendezvous", where the party can gather if forced to separate after a mishap. Amongst Major Rogers' orders are the lines: "Each night you will be told where to meet up if the Indians attack and make us separate." This is a good system. Brady trained his Rangers to assemble at a given distance to the rear of the formation. This will work too. Rendezvous points may be picked enroute or planned before departing. One good idea is to have a rallying point as an alternate for the whole operation. This gives a permanent alternate for the spies to use if they have been separated or the enemy is too near to one of the other rendezvous points.

In practice, if separated, members of the party proceed to the designated rendezvous point and there go into hiding, forming a perimeter to protect the position. This should be automatic.

DANGER AREAS

There are a number of features that are particularly dangerous to the progress of a scout such as passing through an Indian village, crossing a road, or crossing a wide open expanse of grasslands. If at all possible, these should be avoided. If they must be negotiated, then there are precautions that can be taken.

TRAILS: When a road or path is first discovered by the Pilot, the entire body should stop and observe the road for any signs of activity. If it appears safe, then the Pilot should approach cautiously and find out how heavily the path is being used, both to make sure that it is empty and to select a good crossing point. Security should then be sent to both sides to prevent the party being surprised. Once they are in position, the Pilot should cross and make sure the far side is safe. When he signals that all is clear, the main body should cross, followed by the security. Last of all, the Tail should remove any signs of passage. Once all are across, the party should leave the area quickly.

STREAMS AND RIVERS: Small creeks may not present any problem at all, however, larger creeks and rivers are both obstacles and present the additional dangers of either trapping the company or splitting it if the enemy is encountered during the crossing. As with roads, when a watercourse is discovered, the party should stop and observe to make sure there is no hostile activity. When satisfied that all is safe, the Pilot approaches cautiously and makes certain that no one is in sight. He then makes a short scout to determine the best crossing site. Sentries should be posted to protect the crossing and all others take covered positions. The Pilot then strips, bundles his clothing, gear and weapon, and enters the water. First, he checks out the crossing. Next, he crosses the stream and scouts the far side to make sure that all is safe. Once this has been accomplished, he returns to the crossing site and motions one or two people across. These then cross, dress, and become sentries to protect the crossing from the far side. Once all is secured, the remainder of the company is crossed. If necessary, a safety rope can be suspended and safety men can be stationed in the stream to help people, loaded with their gear, to keep their balance. Also, small rafts can be built to float gear and weapons across. Last, the Tail should remove all signs of passage and the party should leave the area immediately.

Because river banks are so susceptible to muddy footprints and damaged foliage, every member of the party must be especially careful not to leave signs of passage on exiting the river.

OPEN AREAS: If at all possible, open prairies, &c., should be crossed at night. In any event, when encountered, a scouting party will halt and observe the whole area carefully. If the enemy does not suspect the scout's presence, enemy sentries may well give their positions away by careless movement. The pilot scouts the crossing first to select the best route. Shallow draws seem to work best because they are rarely watched. Then, sentries are positioned at key points if it seems to be needed. Finally, the leader opens up the formation to a great interval of twenty to thirty paces, then crosses. If there is enemy in the area, they may still be able to cross by crawling.

ENEMY AREAS: Penetrating an enemy line is one of the most difficult things that will be done on any scout. The most secure means is to move slowly, preferably late at night. The scouts listen for enemy positions. They do not make any noise. Crawling is usually best. Four people is about as large a company as is possible to get through a tight line, one or two scouts are much easier. If a gap can be found, a much larger body can be brought through the line.

Entering a village or camp is fairly uncomplicated once the line of sentries is penetrated. Working in the dress of the enemy is not as easy as it might seem, since most spies who try this have had someone try to speak to them in the course of their sojourn into the area. It is probably best to rely on not being seen at all while in the danger area.

STEEP HILLSIDES: If the enemy gets uphill of a small scout, the results can be disastrous. For this reason it is generally best to get off the steep part of a hill, cliff, bluff, &c., as soon as possible. The Leader should scout the hillside first with the company in a safe position. Then they go straight up or straight down, and only then move along the shoulder of the hill or the base of the cliff.

At the Objective

When the target of the scout has been reached, the first step is to create a protected base from where the party can work, reorganize, and rest as needed. The leader should also designate an alternate base, because all too often the base is discovered while a part of the company is absent. An alternate base permits the scout to be reorganized and continued. When the purpose of the scout is to obtain information in a broad area, a number of bases may be established, making smaller scouts from each one.

If the scout is directed at a specific point, enemy camp, or town, &c., then it will be necessary to work someone in close to gather information. Often the best way is to have a team of two people work their way in. One person covers from a reasonably secure position, while the other approaches the enemy. In some circumstances, when there is a long approach, it may be best to use four people. Two cover from long range, one covers from an intermediate position, and the last person works in as close as he can get. In this case the word "cover" means for a person to provide the all-around security for the spy, because he will be too occupied to protect himself. If the enemy spots the endangered man the "cover" fires to make them duck, to give warning, and to create a diversion so the close man can get away. There is still a good argument that one person alone stands the best chance of getting into an enemy area undiscovered and this should be considered.

When the purpose is to watch a point, road, or waterway, this may be best accomplished by establishing a base and a separate observation point, keeping one or two people awake and observing at all times.

For missions that require ambushes; a base is first established and the ambush site scouted. All unnecessary equipment can be left at the base. Security should be placed before the party moves into the ambush site to prepare it. After the ambush has taken place the company returns to the base, secures its gear, reorganizes and leaves the area quickly before the enemy can retaliate. A raid is conducted in much the same manner.

In all cases, the leader of the company should make a personal scout of the target to make certain that the mission will be accomplished as planned. As soon as it is safe to do so, all the information gained from the target should be shared with the whole party.

BREAKS

On any scout it will be necessary to stop movement to rest, drink, fill canteens, let the spies investigate the area, &c. This is one of the most dangerous things that will be done during a scout. More scouts are attacked while halted for a break than at any other time. For this reason, <u>never stop on your own trail to take a break</u>. Double back and watch your back trail; put up a defensive position, get scouts and observation posts out, and protect your break area. Never take a break on your objective, nor on an identifiable terrain feature such as a hilltop, a lone clump of trees, &c. If a meal needs to be cooked, take a break, cook the meal, and then move for a couple more hours before making camp for the night.

For all but the briefest halts, the party should spread out, each member taking cover behind a tree, bush, rock, or other obstruction. Often, if the party is large enough, it is best to take positions in pairs.

If people are to eat, then eat in pairs. While one eats, the other is on guard. If weapons are to be cleaned, only one weapon is taken out of service at a time. If someone must answer a call of nature, another person should go with them and stand guard. The members of the party may rest or nap, but security must be constant. In daylight, at least half the party should be on guard at any time.

OVERNIGHT CAMPS AND BASES

When a camp or base is to be made, a position must be selected carefully that cannot be found or attacked by the enemy. An island in a swamp or a big tree on an inaccessible cliff would be ideal. If at all possible, these should be cold camps. Scouts almost never put up shelters unless it has become a survival situation. For small parties it may be best to huddle around the base of a tree, each facing out, blankets covering everyone, and firelocks across everyone's laps. Another answer is to crawl under some safe bushes or low trees like sumac, lay down in a star formation with everyone's head to the center and feet out. With these two methods, there is the added advantage that everyone is in reach and guards can be awakened without moving around.

Scouts occupy their camp at dark, leaving right at dawn. They do not unpack anything more than necessary and repack it immediately. The party sleeps with their firelocks on them, but not cocked. The rule is not to shoot at an enemy in the dark, since that just gives them a target. Sleeping close together, when someone snores, one of the party can reach over and wake them. One way to prevent snoring is to leave all gear on and sleep on the stomach. In this way, the spy is less likely to roll over. They sleep with their moccasins on and with as much of their gear on their person as possible.

TRACKING

One of the most necessary skills of the scout is the ability to read signs of passage. This becomes simple when they are divided into two categories: top signs and bottom signs. Top signs are from the ankle up and are often the easiest to pick up on the move. These are broken twigs, tufts of hair or fiber, bruise marks where someone steadied himself on a sapling, broken spider webs, and bent grasses. Bottom signs are almost always tracks, scuff marks, or overturned pebbles.

The tracker must know his territory intimately. He must know how long it takes for grass to stand back up in the springtime and how long a footprint will stay moist in that type of soil. He can judge the size and weight of the person or animal that left a track by comparing it with his own, but he relies on an experience factor to tell him how long ago it was left and what the conditions of passage were.

If the trail is lost, it often can be relocated by making casts in an organized manner out from the last known track. Roads, paths, streams, and areas of soft ground are ideal for this. Go completely around the area where the trail was lost, working in ever widening squares or circles until the trail is found again.

Tracking an enemy is dangerous because when you find him, he shoots at you. The tracker must be protected while he is concentrating on a trail. The tracker cannot also be the pilot.

Everyone on a scout must be aware of tracking skills, because anyone can discover tracks and the company will leave tracks that could potentially lead the enemy to them.

FIGHTING

The scout must avoid being forced into a fight with the enemy at all costs. If contact is made with an enemy force, however, the scout must react violently and without hesitation. Never do what the enemy wants you to do. Instead, either break and run immediately, reorganizing at your rendezvous point and set up an ambush, or attack violently even though outnumbered.

With single shot firelocks, it is best to fight in pairs so that one member of the pair is always loaded. Fire from behind trees or rocks, and then move quickly. It must be practiced. Volley firing means that everyone is unloaded at once--- not always a good idea.

The scout should take cover immediately to return fire. "Tree", the term often used in old journals, means taking cover behind a tree. Often we tend to return fire standing up and in the open. Robert Rogers wrote: "kneel down, lie down, hide behind a tree", for a reason. The scout must be careful not to fire from the same place around a tree or rock, time after time. He fires from under a bush once, around the other side of the tree the next, and then kneels and fires from over the bush the third shot. Elsewise, the enemy will see him shoot and wait for him to put his head back out in the same place. This takes some practice to take cover far enough back from the tree to permit a few firing points.

Many times we stand in the open firing because of the ease of loading. The scout should train himself to load kneeling, lying down, on a horse, waist deep in water, and on the dead run. Often the secret to loading in these conditions is to pour the powder into the hand, rather than try to use the powder measure, and then dropping the ball in unpatched. The frontiersmen's practice of patching with leather, linen, or bees nests generally requires a smaller ball anyway.

If all else fails, a covering party may be left behind to allow the main body to escape. In any case, once a fight begins, scouts must fight to some objective. The leader designates the point that will be the objective. Then the party must fight their way to that point. Scouts must remember that their purpose is to get free of the enemy and continue their mission.

AMBUSHES

One of the best uses of scouts is to bring back a prisoner. For this reason, ambushes are a very common occurrence in the course of a scout. Members of the company should develop a set of standard ambush plans that can be put in place without any talking. Thus, it should be decided who should fire the first shot before ever going into enemy country and not at the ambush site. Furthermore, decisions should be made as to who will be on security, who will guard prisoners, &c.

It is difficult to select an ambush formation ahead of time because this is largely dictated by the terrain. Very common formations are the Line, "V","T", and Area ambushes. If a company is to remain as a unit for a while, it would be wise to practice all of these often.

Line: The most basic of all ambushes, the ambushers are all on the same side of the killing zone. Security should be placed to flanks and rear.

"V": Extremely common in Indian wars, the Indians used this to ambush the withdrawing English troops after Ft. William Henry, and Brady used it near Honia on the Cuyahoga River. The "V" works best when a path goes through a steep sided valley or gully. The ambushers are on both sides, close at the head of the enemy column. The ambushers fire down into the enemy.

"T": Also called the bloody nose ambush, the ambushers take positions directly in front of the enemy line of march. Braddock led his army into a "T" ambush.

Area Ambush: This is typical of the Indian hunting party. A number of small ambush sites are spread out over an area and the ambush is triggered at what is hopefully the most advantageous moment. The target may then be ambushed multiple times before they can escape. This is very good when the enemy can enter the area from any side.

In selecting an ambush site, care must be taken that the enemy is contained in the killing zone and that there is no cover from which the enemy could hide and return fire. It is often best if there is some obstruction so that the enemy cannot charge into the ambushers.

Fig. 4 **Line** Ambush

Fig. 5 "V" Ambush

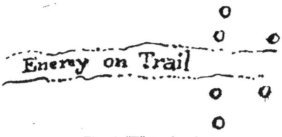

Fig. 6 "T" Ambush

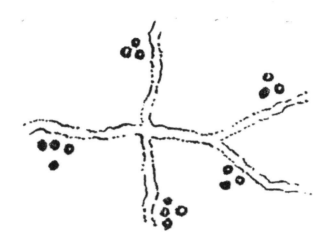

Fig. 7 **Area** Ambush

The steps of setting up an ambush should be something along the lines of: First, the leader searches the area for signs of enemy passage and an adequate site; Next, place security to make sure you are not surprised while setting the ambush up; Then, prepare and occupy the position; wait for the enemy; set the ambush off; reorganize, redistribute loads and ammunition and secure prisoners; and finally, leave the area at once.

Many leaders will not let any member of the party step into the killing zone for fear that their tracks will tip the enemy off.

The hasty ambush is a very worthwhile tactic that all scouts should be familiar with. Used when trackers are closing in or when contact is imminent from a hostile force, the scouts take cover quickly, and at least one person automatically assumes the position of rear security. When the enemy comes in range, they are fired on before they have a chance to read the tracks and decide that an ambush is likely. This tactic keeps trackers honest.

The best protection against an enemy ambuscade is to detect it before getting into its kill zone. There are a number of tell-tale signs that a pilot may look for. Lanes for firing that are cut by the ambushers, tracks in unnatural directions, and drying vegetation used to hide the firing positions are three such signs. Often poorly hidden ambushers give their positions away by movement or failure to make sure that all their weapons and clothing are subdued. Pilots should become increasingly cautious when approaching a site that would facilitate an enemy ambush.

If a scouting party ends up in an enemy ambuscade, they must attack directly toward the ambushers instantly without waiting for any command. Quick, violent action is all that will save a person in a killing zone. The best answer is an alert pilot that can detect an ambush before the company is in danger.

ENEMY TRACKERS

Probably the greatest hazard to the scouting party is the enemy tracker. Once the enemy knows that scouts are working in the area, their logical course of action is to send out larger scouting parties of their own to find the trail. Often the first warning they have of the scouting party's presence is a carelessly left track. The best remedy is to never leave any signs of passage.

Passive measures would include selecting the best surface to leave as few tracks as possible. Scouts walk in leaves rather than on sand or dirt that will leave a track that is hard to erase. When they can walk on downed trees, roots, or rocks, they do so. The spy must cover his trail as he goes. When they take a break, they double back and watch their back trail. The first time an enemy tracker finds they have doubled back, his speed drops drastically because he must then watch out for ambushes.

If a scout has reason to believe that he is being tracked, he may lay false trails and cover his tracks especially well. He uses creeks to walk in, but takes care that he does not make a trail when he leaves the water. He can go up the steepest hill he can find and then lay a hasty ambush near the top or he can loop around to get behind the enemy trackers.

MESSENGERS

From time to time it will be necessary to send messengers back to the commander as important information is discovered. If there is a possibility that messengers will be needed, they should be planned for before the party ever leaves its base. This is one of the advantages of a large party. The scout selected to be the messenger must be self-reliant and possibly the best woodsman in the party. The messenger will have the best chance of avoiding detection and successfully delivering the message if he travels alone. If at all possible, the messenger should be given a verbal message and he should repeat it for the leader to make sure that he has the information correctly. This way, should the enemy discover him they will find no written material on him and they will have no indication that he was a messenger. He can say he was lost or separated. The messenger should return by the most secure route, not the fastest.

Survival and Health

A scout must survive in order to accomplish his mission. Survival is a state of mind. If a person does not let themselves be defeated, he will survive. Survival requires three things; warmth, water, and food, in that order.

Clothing should be of wool, linen, hemp and silk. Cotton is not a good survival choice. In cold and wet conditions, choose wool and silk.

The most dangerous hazard is hypothermia, also called exposure. This occurs when the body cannot maintain its temperature. If the party can stay reasonably dry and protected, a little discomfort can be borne. Essentially, dry is warm. People in the wilderness must protect their dry clothing. They should consider removing all or part of the clothing in order to have something dry to put on when they stop moving. If rain is expected, they should take the extra time to construct dry, weatherproof shelters. If the scout becomes wet and cold, movement will keep him alive. There is a test a scout can perform on himself to find out if hypothermia has gone too far. Touch the pinky finger to the thumb. If you cannot do this, it has become an emergency. <u>If it becomes a survival situation, build a fire, go modern, and go for help.</u>

Water is the next most important requirement. On a hot or dry day, lack of water can bring on a heat injury such as heat cramps, heat exhaustion, or even heat stroke. People on scouts should drink their fill whenever they have the chance. The leader should have everyone fill their canteens at every spring or stream they come across and at the same time fill themselves up. If there are any doubts about its safety, water should be purified. As long as the urine is clear and copious, you are not dehydrated.

Since it would be rare that anyone would exceed a month on a scout, foods are not a major factor in survival. Most of us can survive up to forty days on water alone. As a general rule, however, the spy should never eat all his food. When rations begin to get short, he should eat half of the remainder each day. Eating just prior to going to sleep will help a person sleep warmer.

Poisonous plants can be a hazard. On a scout, people should not be so close to survival that they should need to eat any wild foods. If it becomes necessary, however, and there is any doubt, do not eat it. Irritants such as poison ivy and poison oak are another matter. The scout must learn to recognize them and avoid them. In the dark, it is wise to check any trees that they are going to sleep against or use as a cover, for climbing vines--it is not worth the risk.

Poisonous animals and insects are a much overrated danger. In fact, they are more of a nuisance than a real hazard. In most cases, a healthy adult will survive the bite of a poisonous snake or spider without treatment. Still, if scouting in a snake hazard area, there are some safety rules that should be remembered:

1. Do not put a foot or hand in a place that cannot be seen.
2. Do not reach into holes.
3. When turning rocks or logs over, keep the object between the person and any possible hazard.
4. Look before sitting down.
5. Do not step over obstacles, like logs, without looking.

If bitten, get the victim quickly to medical attention. Do not treat the bite. Almost all traditional treatments are more dangerous than the bite itself. The party should try to identify the snake or bring it with them, but not at the expense of speed in getting medical attention. The victim should be gotten to medical help quickly, but safely.

There are also a number of insects that are more of a bother than a danger but can, without a doubt, influence the scout's efficiency. These are the mosquito, gnat, biting fly, tick, chigger, scorpion, &c. Humans just do not cope well with the habits of insects. There is no sure way to protect oneself from these terrors, but there are a few things that can help. No insect repellant is foolproof. Most, applied to the skin, are soon sweated off or simply worn away. Applied to the openings of the scout's clothing --- neck, button holes, wrists, hems, &c., will keep the insects out for a little while longer, but must be reapplied frequently. A neck cloth heavily saturated with an herbal decoction of pennyroyal, lavender, and rosemary, under a wide brimmed hat has worked as well as anything. Most insects are attracted to light colors, especially mosquitoes, so dark colored clothing is in order. It would seem that the best protection is a combination of some repellant, dark clothing, hats, and then just ignoring the little buggers.

Fires can sometimes be a necessary evil. When keeping warm becomes a necessity, the best answer seems to be to keep fires to an absolute minimum. Use a fire as infrequently as possible and make the fire as small as possible. If a fire is needed to cook, keep it small, cook, and then leave the area. Try to keep cooking fires to a single meal, such as noon for example. Try to limit fires to daylight and use smoke free fuels such as shag bark hickory bark.

At night, if a fire is to be used for warmth, it may be built in a hole about the size of half a man's head over which scout huddles with the fire between his legs, covering both himself and the fire with his blanket, ala Simon Kenton. This can be done with a single candle, but, candles are so scarce and expensive on the frontier that this use would be unlikely. If a larger fire is to be built, consider surrounding the fire with half-faced shelters or building a reflector to keep the light from being seen. Guards must be placed outside the circle of light or else they will peer blindly into the night.

Shelter is another comfort that should be done without if at all possible. If they must be used, scouts should keep shelters as small and low to the ground as possible. The use of as many natural materials as possible will help to make the shelter unobtrusive.

Each person on a scout should carry the minimum items for his personal survival in the wilderness on his person where they will not be separated from him. For example, a spy might carry a penny knife, flint, steel and char, and a small compass in a pouch, on the belt to his breechclout. With these, he could survive almost anything.

It would be a good idea for anyone interested in scouting to get a good course in first aid. Broken bones and severe cuts are always a possibility. The key to survival, still, is to keep ones head. Common sense will get the scout out of almost anything and he is not defeated until he gives up.

LOGISTICS

Most of us are not very realistic in our choice of the materials of scouting. For some reason there is more interest in filling our packs than there is in filling our list of skills. Consequently we are over armed, over equipped, and over fed. On the scout, the barest minimum is the best answer.

Food: On a scout, it is often best to plan only cold trail foods such as jerky, parched corn, biscuits, cheese, &c. Cooking is an unnecessary risk. No one will starve to death on a scout. Limit rations to a handful or so, per day.

Water: Another problem altogether is water. Everyone should carry some form of canteen and a drinking cup. Fill canteens at every available water source. Water purification devices or tablets are a good idea if the water is questionable. Boiling is not usually an option on a scout.

Firelocks and Ammunition: Since the purpose of a weapon on a scout is for protection, all things being equal, a smoothbore fowler or musket would seem to be the best choice. However, on the frontier most people do not have a choice of weapons and we go on a scout with whatever our household weapon has been. The scout must pay attention, however, to the shiny metal and wood of the firelock. The weapon should be dark and dull finished if possible. History books are full of accounts of people found and ambushes detected by the shine of the metal on a weapon. A couple dozen balls should be sufficient ammunition, along with a pound of powder in the horn and half dozen flints. Bullet molds, lead and ladles are extra weight that probably should be left behind. Spare parts and tools may also be more of a liability than an asset. On a scout a person must be light in order to move silently. Generally, having the horn and pouch high and close to the body is the most silent. If the horn is on the same side as the rifle it tends to connect with a loud clack at inopportune times.

Clothing: The most practical arrangement for scouting seems to be what Washington described as an Indian walking suit; a combination of a hunting shirt and leggings with shoe packs or moccasins on the feet. A brimmed hat should be carried, but it can be folded and stuffed in the hunting shirt when not needed. A neck cloth helps cover the shine of human skin at the neck and chest, can be used to muffle coughs and sneezes, to cool one down, or to serve as a bandage. The belt or sash must be wide enough to carry the load of knife and tomahawk comfortably. Either trousers or breechcloth work well. A second shirt worn under the hunting shirt is usually a good idea. It can be removed and carried in the blanket roll. In cold weather, a waistcoat can be added. Leg ties should be unadorned as even small white beads or quill work show up a long way off in the dark woods. Nothing should dangle about the body, no noggins, no powder measurers, and no neck knives. If the canteen can go inside the pack or haversack, then so much the better. Both packs and haversacks have their good points. Packs are generally easier to carry, but a haversack does not have to be taken off to get at ones ration. On a scout, the loads should be so light that either works comfortably. The bedroll may be only a match coat or a half blanket. Members of the scout can huddle together to keep warm. Knife and tomahawk need to be so placed that they will not hit the powder horn or firelock and make noise.

COMMON MISTAKES

Before closing, it would be wise to look at some of the common mistakes seen on scouts. We all learn from mistakes, either our own or the mistakes of others. If the scout survives them, the only thing wrong with a mistake is if he fails to learn from it.

The most common mistake seen is that of moving too fast. When the party moves faster than it should, the first thing that happens is the security breaks down. The Pilot and Tail cannot do their jobs and no one can adequately cover their sectors.   Generally, this is a beginner's mistake.

Another mistake is going out on a scout too heavily loaded.   This makes it impossible to move silently and greatly increases fatigue. Tired scouts make mistakes. It is far better to do without some creature comforts in order to keep the load as light as possible.

We pay so much attention to our walnut dyed hunting shirts and then wear beaded garters and a quilled knife sheath that can be seen a quarter mile away. Sleeves rolled up and a bare head can undo all the good that has been done by the dark colors of the Indian walking suit.

Inexperienced scouts tend to pick the easiest route to and from the target.   This is exactly where the enemy is looking for them.

The final big problem is the failure to control noise. We are just not used to living without speaking out loud and walking everywhere on our tiptoes. Our voices carry, even when we think we are being quiet. The only answer is not to talk at all. But it is more than this. We are used to arming and equipping ourselves for the shooting match and the parade field.   No one gives a second thought about having a loading block or a powder measure hanging on the strap of the shooting pouch. Go on a scout. How many times do you hear the sound of a powder horn hitting some other hard object? How about tin cups?

AFTER THE SCOUT

When the scout has finished and the party has returned to the safety of the main body, fort, or army, the most important thing to accomplish is to give the information to the people who need it. It usually works best if the entire party is present when the information is given. Every person on the scout will have seen different things. All of these may have had some importance. All need to be present for the telling of the story unless there is some unusual reason why one or more should be excluded.

Finally, it would be a good idea to talk over the progress of the scout with the members of the party while everything is still fresh in everyone's minds. There are many lessons to be learned and each member will have picked up on something different. This is especially important if you intend to continue to make scouts together.

POSTSCRIPT

In all, the picture of scouting that is drawn here is one of the Scout making austere uncomfortable movement through the roughest terrain while seeking an enemy who is looking for him. The rewards are that few people can do it at all, and fewer still scout well. The skills can be learned, and it is unlikely that anyone is born a good scout in any culture. Most scouts have taught themselves. The two most important attributes to start with are common sense and the powers of observation. Thus, when on a trek, if a prospective scout sees a person wearing a blue and white checkered hunting shirt and it stands out in the woods, he learns not to wear one. The same with ranger green jackets with pewter buttons. If the sun reflecting off the bare forehead of an Indian gave warning of an impending ambush, then he knows to cover his own forehead, and if he can hear other people's guns thwack their powder horns, he moves his powder horn to a better place. Some things just have to be tried. A Scout should try to sleep sitting up while leaning against a tree to find out how it works for him, and try walking, leaving as few tracks as possible.

There is no substitute for time in the woods. Moving slowly and silently, threading one's way through blackberries, being acutely aware of every living creature around you, takes endless practice. These are not the skills of the longhunter who goes out and lives off the land for a year or two while accumulating hides and meat for market. Scouting is the specific skill of locating and reporting information about the enemy and the land. It is often a war time skill. A good hunter has much of this same knowledge, but hasn't the element of fear that drives a scout to see his movement as a sojourn into a hostile environment. A longhunter may encounter friendly Indians --- the scout never will. It completely changes the nature of the game. Were you to become a competent scout you must divorce yourself from all thought of comfort and safety and think fear...think alone...and think silent.

Patrol Tips

1. A backdrop, such as a dark bush, may be as good as a bush in front of you to hide your position.

2. Keep a cough remedy, such as bitterroot, where you can reach it --- a nervous cough can be embarrassing when you are close to an enemy.

3. The knot on the neck cloth can be used to stifle a sneeze or a cough.

4. Be careful what fabrics you choose. For example, canvas gaiters are noisy --- maybe not noisy enough for the enemy to hear you, but the sound of twigs scraping them drowns out the sound of the enemy or animal that you are listening for.

5. Keep a survival pouch on you at all times – enough to get you through in a pinch. For example, a knife and a fire making kit.

6. Do not be too quick to fire your weapon. The Indians are afraid of a loaded firelock, but they are not afraid of an unloaded firelock. Also, the enemy may not have been sure that they saw you and when you fire, you confirm the sighting.

7. Do not smoke on a scout, not for any reason. Tobacco smoke travels a long way and the signs of lit tobacco are nearly impossible to hide at night.

8. Let half your breath out before you whisper. This will make much less noise.

9. Never move directly on top of a ridge, this is where the enemy will move, there are often trails there and you will be silhouetted. Instead move on the shoulder of the ridge (military crest).

10. Do not take a break or camp near a rushing stream. The sound of the stream will mask the sounds of enemy movement.

11. Be careful about grabbing vegetation as you move. Some types of bark, crab apple is one of them, are covered with a dust-like substance that has an affinity for body oils and you will leave a hand print that a tracker can see. Leaves that have been grabbed show bruise marks. Trees and saplings that are used as handholds can shake giving your position away.

12. Do not take a weapon with a sling on a scout. Slings make noise, they snag things, and you will not spend much time with the weapon slung on a scout.

13. Never set a pattern, but do it differently every time.

14. Leather or cloth wrap everything you carry. Noise is a killer.

Sign Language

It is a good idea to develop a system of communicating silently within a scout. Many people all over the world have developed sign languages for this purpose or others. An abbreviated system will work well. Some terms that should be included are:

Circle hand above head
Fig. 8 Assemble

Fig. 9 Go

Fig. 10 Come

Fig. 11 Halt

Fig. 12 Down

Fig. 13 Up

Wag hand back & forth

Fig. 14 Question

Fig. 15 Cover (Him, me, &c.)

Fig. 16 Man (person)

Fig. 17 Woman

Fig. 18 Animal

Point to knife

Fig. 19 American

Rub paint on face

Fig. 20 Indian

Long nose

Fig. 21 French

Fig. 22 English

Fig. 23 Stream

Fig. 24 Trail

Fig. 25 Under

Fig. 26 Across

Fig. 27 Danger

Fig. 28 All clear

Break a stick

Fig. 29 Break

Fig. 30 Eat

Fig. 31 Drink

Fig. 32 Sleep

Fist pumps to side

Fig. 33 Ambush

Upraised arm drops

Fig. 34 Fire (Shoot)

EQUIPAGE FOR A SCOUT
OF UNDETERMINED LENGTH

Clothing

Hat

Neck Cloth

Hunting Shirt

Waistcoat

Belt or sash

Breech clout or breeches

Leggings

Stockings

Leg ties

Moccasins or shoe packs

Carried

Firelock

Pouch

Horn

Tomahawk

Knife

Blanket or matchcoat

Canteen

Spare moccasins

Food

Paper & Pencil

Haversack, pack, or wallet

Powder measure

Worm or string

Vent pick

Pickering's tool

Balls (24+)

Flints (6+)

Spare leathers or leads

Tow or rag

Fire kit & candle

Awl

Food quiver for rations

Possible

Map

Compass

String or rope

Testament

Sewing Kit

Mitts

Ball starter

Ram rod puller

Canvas sheet

Cup & spoon

Salt

Waistcoat

Do Not Favor Us With:

Tobacco	Bullet molds
Alcohol	Lead & Ladle
Musical instruments	Mainspring
Skillets	Mainspring vise

❖ Everything should be in dark colors. No beadwork, quillwork, or bright metal – ANYWHERE!

❖ Go light; make everything serve two or more purposes, substitute skill for weight.

❖ The load must be compact and high. Nothing dangles on the outside.

Major Robert Rogers
His Rules for Ranging Service

I.

All Rangers are to be subject to the rules and articles of war; to appear at roll-call every evening of their own parade, equipped, each with a fire-lock, sixty rounds of powder and ball, and a hatchet, at which time an officer from each company is to inspect the same, to see they are in order, so as to be read on any emergency to march at a minute's warning; & before they are dismissed the necessary guards are to drafted, and scouts for the next day appointed.

II.

Whenever you are ordered out to the enemies forts or frontiers for discoveries, if your number be small, march in single file, keeping at such a distance from each other as to prevent one shot killing two men, sending one man, or more, forward, and the like on each side, at the distance of twenty yards from the main body, if the ground you march over will admit of it, to give the signal to the officer of the approach of the enemy, and their number &c.

III.

If you march over marshes or soft ground, change your position, and march abreast of each other, to prevent the enemy from tracking, (as they would do if you marched in a single file) till you get over such ground, and then resume your former order, and march till it is quite dark before you encamp, which do, if possible, on a piece of ground that may afford your sentries the advantage of seeing and hearing the enemy at some considerable distance, keeping one half of your whole party awake alternately through the night.

IV.

Some time before you come to the place you would reconnoiter, make a stand, and send one or two men, in whom you can confide, to look out the best ground for making your observations.

V.

If you have to good fortune to take any prisoners, keep them separate, till they are examined, and in your return take a different route that in which you went out, that you may the better discover any party in your rear, and have an opportunity, if their strength be superior to yours, to alter your course, or disperse, as circumstances may require.

VI.

If you march in a large body of three or four hundred, with a design to attack the enemy, divide your party into three columns, each headed by a proper officer, and let these columns march in a single files, the columns to the right and left keeping at twenty yards distance or more from that of the center, if the ground will admit, and let proper guards be kept in the front and rear, and suitable flanking parties at a due distance as before directed, with orders to halt on all eminences, to take a view of the surrounding ground, to prevent your being ambuscaded, and to notify the approach or retreat of the enemy, that proper dispositions may be made for attacking, defending, &c. And if the enemy approach in your front on level ground, form a front of your three columns or main body with the advanced guard, keeping out your flanking parties, as if you were marching under the command of trusty officers, to prevent the enemy from pressing hard on either of your wings, or surrounding you, which is the usual method of the savages, if their number will admit of it; and be careful likewise to support and strengthen your rear-guard.

VII.

If you are obliged to receive the enemy's fire, fall, or squat down, till it is over, then rise and discharge at them. If their main body is equal to yours, extended yourselves occasionally; but if superior, be careful to support and strengthen your flanking parties, to make them equal with theirs, that if possible you may repulse them to their main body, in which case push upon them with the greatest resolution, with equal force in each flank and in the center, observing to keep at a due distance from each other, and advance from tree to tree, with one half of the party before the other ten or twelve yards. If the enemy push upon you, let your front fire and fall down, and then let your rear advance thro' them and do the like, by which time those who before were in front will be ready to discharge again, and repeat the same alternately, as occasion shall require; by this means you will keep up such a constant fire, that the enemy will not be able easily to break your order, or gain your ground.

VIII.

If you oblige the enemy to retreat, be careful, in your pursuit of them, to keep out your flanking parties, and prevent them from gaining eminences, or rising grounds, in which case they would perhaps be able to rally and repulse you in their turn.

IX.

If you are obliged to retreat, let the front of your whole party fire and fall back, till the rear hath done the same, making for the best ground you can; by this means you will oblige the enemy to pursue you, if they do it at all, in the face of a constant fire.

X.

If the enemy is so superior that you are in danger of being surrounded by them, let the whole body disperse, and take a different road to the place of rendezvous appointed for that evening, which must every morning be altered and fixed for the evening ensuing, in order to bring the whole party, or as many of them as possible, together, after any separation that may happen in the day; but if you should yourselves into a square, or if in the woods, a circle is best, and, if possible, make a stand till the darkness of the night favors your escape.

XI.

If your rear is attacked, the main body and flankers must face about to the right or left, as occasion shall require, and form themselves to oppose the enemy, as before directed; and the same method must be observed, if attacked in either of your flanks, by which means you will always make a rear of one of your flankguards.

XII.

If you determine to rally after a retreat, in order to make a fresh stand against the enemy, by all means endeavor to do it on the most rising ground you can come at, which will give you greatly the advantage in point of situation, and enable you to repulse superior numbers.

XIII.

In general when pushed upon by the enemy, reserve your fire till they approach very near, which will then put them into the greater surprise and consternation, and give you advantage.

XIV.

When you encamp at night, fix your sentries in such a manner as not to be relieved from the main body till morning, profound secrecy and silence being often of the last importance in these cases. Each sentry, therefore, should consist of six men, two of whom must be constantly alert, and when relieved by their fellows, it should be done without noise; and in case those on duty see or hear anything, which alarms them, they are not to speak, but one of them is silently to retreat, and acquaint the commanding officer thereof, that proper dispositions may be made; and all occasional sentries should be fixed in like manner.

XV.

At the first dawn of day, awake your whole detachment; that being the time when the savages choose to fall upon their enemies, you should by all means be in readiness to receive them.

XVI.

If the enemy should be discovered by your detachments in the morning, and their numbers are superior to yours, and a victory doubtful, you should not attack them till the evening, as then they will not know your numbers, and if you are repulsed, your retreat will be favored by the darkness of the night.

XVII.

Before you leave your encampment, send out small parties to scout round it, to see if there be any appearance or trace of an enemy that might have been near you during the night.

XVIII.

When you stop for refreshment, choose some spring or rivulet if you can, and dispose your party so as not to be surprised, posting proper guards and sentries at a due distance, and let a small party waylay the path you came in, lest the enemy should be pursuing.

XIX.

If, in your return, you have to cross rivers, avoid the usual fords as much as possible, lest the enemy should have discovered, and be there expecting you.

XX.

If you have to pass by lakes, keep at some distance from the edge of the water, lest, in case of an ambuscade, or an attack from the enemy, when in the situation, your retreat should be cut off.

XX.

When you return from a scout, and come near our forts, avoid the usual roads, and avenues thereto, lest the enemy should have headed you, when almost exhausted with fatigues.

XXI.

When you pursue any party that has been near our forts or encampments, follow not directly in their tracks; lest you should be discovered by their rear-guards, who, at such a time, would be most alert; but endeavor, by a different route, to head and meet them in some narrow pass, or lay in ambush to receive them when and where they least expect.

XXII.

If you are to embark in canoes, battoes, or otherwise, by water, choose the evening for the time of your embarkation, as you will then have the whole night before you, to pass undiscovered by any parties of the enemy, on hills, or other places, which command a prospect of the lake or river you are upon.

XXIII.

In paddling or rowing, give orders that the boat or canoe next the sternmost, wait for her, and the third for the second, and the fourth for the third, and so on, to prevent separation, and that you may be ready to assist each other on any emergency.

XXIV.

Appoint one man in each boat to look out for fires, on adjacent shores, from the numbers and size of which you may form some judgment of the number that kindles them, and whether you are able to attack them or not.

XXV.

If you find the enemy encamped near the banks of a river, or lake, which you imagine they will attempt to cross for their security upon being attacked, leave a detachment of your party on the opposite shore to receive them, while, with the remainder, you surprise them, having them between you and the lake or river.

XXVI.

If you cannot satisfy yourself as to the enemy's number and strength, from their fire, &c. conceal your boats at some distance, and ascertain their number by reconnoitering party; when they embark, or march, in the morning, marking the course they steer, &c. When you may pursue, ambush, and attack them, or let them pass, as prudence shall direct you. In general, however, that you may not be discovered by the enemy on the lakes or rivers at a great distance, it is safest to lay by, with your boats and party concealed all day, without noise or show, and to pursue your intended route by night; and whether you go by land or water, give out parole and countersigns, in order to know one another in the dark, and likewise appoint a station for every man to repair to, in case of any accident that may separate you.

INDEX

Printed in Great Britain
by Amazon